When Butterflies Cross the Sky
THE MONARCH BUTTERFLY MIGRATION
Sharon Katz Cooper
by Joshua S. Brunet
D0185604
Cardiff Libraries
www.cardiff.gov.uk/libraries
CARDIFF
CAERDYDD
Llyfrgelloedd Caerdydd
ACC. No: 05037803

Raintree is an imprint of Capstone Global Library Limited, a company incorporated in England and Wales having its registered office at 7 Pilgrim Street, London, EC4V 6LB – Registered company number: 6695582

www.raintree.co.uk
myorders@raintree.co.uk

With thanks to our advisers for their expertise, research and advice:

Wendy Caldwell, Program Coordinator, Monarch Joint Venture
University of Minnesota, Twin Cities, USA

Terry Flaherty, PhD, Professor of English
Minnesota State University, Mankato, USA

Editorial Credits
Jill Kalz, editor; Lori Bye, designer; Nathan Gassman, art director; Laura Manthe, production specialist

ISBN 978 1 4062 9341 8
20 19 18 17 16
10 9 8 7 6 5 4 3 2 1

British Library Cataloguing in Publication Data
A full catalogue record for this book is available from the British Library.

Photo Credits
The illustrations in this book were created with acrylics.
Image Credit: Shutterstock: ekler, 3 (map)

Printed in China.

EDITOR'S NOTE: There are usually four generations of monarch butterflies in a 12-month period. The first three generations live for two to six weeks each. But the fourth generation is special. It lives for up to nine months. It is the generation that migrates south in the autumn. This book tells the story of a fourth-generation monarch butterfly from the United States.

Monarch butterflies weigh less than a paper clip. Yet every year they migrate up to 4,023 kilometres (2,500 miles) from the United States and southern Canada. Butterflies west of the Rocky Mountains fly to the coast of California. Butterflies east of the Rocky Mountains fly to Mexico. No other butterfly travels so far. Flying about 48 kilometres (30 miles) every day, monarch butterflies complete the journey to Mexico in about two months. Why is this journey so important to them?

Flutter, flutter! Flutter, flutter! The butterfly flits from flower to flower. The sun is warm on her wings. She sips nectar with her straw-like tongue and fills herself up. The sweet food will give her energy for the long flight ahead.

Autumn arrives. The days get shorter. A cool breeze swishes the leaves.

The butterfly knows it's time to head south. She cannot survive the long months of freezing weather here. She needs a warmer winter home. So do the other monarch butterflies.

The butterfly joins hundreds of other monarchs in the sky. Air currents lift her, so she doesn't have to beat her wings all the time. She saves energy by gliding.

The butterfly will stop to drink nectar and to rest. But she cannot rest for long. She's racing against the cold weather. Even though she's never made this journey before, her body knows the way.

The butterfly's journey is dangerous. She may not find enough food to eat. She may become too tired to finish her journey. Birds and other animals may try to eat her. Bad weather may slow or stop her. She cannot fly in the rain, and she cannot fly if it gets too cold.

Finally, about two months later, the butterfly reaches her winter home. The mountains of central Mexico are perfect for her. The air is cold but not quite freezing. The butterfly can rest and save her energy throughout the winter.

The butterfly settles onto a tree. Millions of other butterflies do the same. Blankets of orange and black butterflies cover the trees.

The butterfly is safe for now. She spends the winter resting, clinging to the trees. The trees protect her from predators and bad weather. She drinks water occasionally, but she does not eat much. She stored lots of energy on her journey south.

At the end of February the butterfly mates. Then it's time to find someplace to lay her eggs. There is no milkweed in the mountains of Mexico. The butterfly needs milkweed. It's the only plant on which she will lay her eggs.

The butterfly knows she has to fly north again. Her journey isn't quite over. She has one last job to do.

The butterfly leaves Mexico with millions of other monarchs. She lays her eggs on milkweed plants as she heads north. When she has laid her eggs, her long journey ends, and she dies.

After a few days, a tiny, hungry caterpillar hatches from each egg.

The caterpillars eat lots of milkweed. In about two weeks, they're old enough to start changing into adults. They shed their skin and harden into a bright green chrysalis. Great changes take place inside.

About 10 days later, new butterflies crawl out. They will soon fly away in search of food, a mate and the warm summer sun.

Monarch Butterfly Fast Facts

Scientific name: *Danaus plexippus*

Adult weight (average): roughly 0.6 grams (0.02 ounces)

Adult size: 10 centimetres (3.9 inches) wide

Diet of butterflies: nectar, sipped through a straw-like tongue called a proboscis

Diet of caterpillars: milkweed

Identifying spot: males have a small dark spot on the inside part of their rear wings; females don't

Number of eggs: females lay about 700 eggs

Size of eggs: the size of a pinhead

Lifespan of migratory monarchs: 7 to 9 months

Length of migration: up to 4,023 kilometres (2,500 miles)

Comprehension Questions

1. Why is it important for monarch butterflies to migrate every autumn?
2. Describe the dangers monarch butterflies face on their migration journey.
3. Explain what the map on page 3 shows.

Glossary

caterpillar larva that changes into a butterfly or moth; a caterpillar is the second life stage of a butterfly

chrysalis third stage of a butterfly; "pupa" is another word for chrysalis

current movement of air in a certain direction

mate join together to produce young; a mate is also the male or female partner of a pair of animals

milkweed plant with milky juice and pointed pods; monarch butterflies will only lay their eggs on milkweed

nectar sweet liquid found in many flowers

predator animal that hunts other animals

proboscis long tube-shaped mouthpart

shed drop or let go of

survive stay alive

Read More

Butterflies (Great Migrations), Laura Marsh (National Geographic Society, 2010)

Eggs, Legs and Wings (Nature Cycles), Shannon Knudsen (Raintree, 2011)

Grow Your Own Butterfly Farm (Grow It Yourself!), John Malam (Raintree, 2012)

Websites

www.bbc.co.uk/nature/life/Monarch_(butterfly)
Learn more about monarch butterflies, and watch some amazing videos on the BBC website.

www.nationalgeographic.com/animals/bugs/monarch-butterfly
Find out about the mass migrations that the monarch butterflies take to warmer climates every year.

www.ukbutterflies.co.uk
Search for monarch butterflies on this website to see hundreds of photographs documenting the life of a monarch butterfly in the UK and across the world.

Index

LOOK OUT FOR ALL THE BOOKS IN THE SERIES: